SHAPING THE DEBATE

Defining and Discussing
CLIMATE CHANGE

Christy Mihaly

A Division of

Before Reading: *Building Background Knowledge and Vocabulary*

Building background knowledge can help children process new information and build upon what they already know. Before reading a book, it is important to tap into what children already know about the topic. This will help them develop their vocabulary and increase their reading comprehension.

Questions and Activities to Build Background Knowledge:

1. Look at the front cover of the book and read the title. What do you think this book will be about?
2. What do you already know about this topic?
3. Take a book walk and skim the pages. Look at the table of contents, photographs, captions, and bold words. Did these text features give you any information or predictions about what you will read in this book?

Vocabulary: *Vocabulary Is Key to Reading Comprehension*

Use the following directions to prompt a conversation about each word.

- Read the vocabulary words.
- What comes to mind when you see each word?
- What do you think each word means?

Vocabulary Words:
- acidic
- assess
- climate
- developed
- droughts
- emissions
- federal
- greenhouse gases
- polar
- regional
- violates
- wetlands

During Reading: *Reading for Meaning and Understanding*

To achieve deep comprehension of a book, children are encouraged to use close reading strategies. During reading, it is important to have children stop and make connections. These connections result in deeper analysis and understanding of a book.

 Close Reading a Text

During reading, have children stop and talk about the following:

- Any confusing parts
- Any unknown words
- Text to text, text to self, text to world connections
- The main idea in each chapter or heading

Encourage children to use context clues to determine the meaning of any unknown words. These strategies will help children learn to analyze the text more thoroughly as they read.

When you are finished reading this book, turn to page 46 for **Text-Dependent Questions** and an **Extension Activity**.

TABLE OF CONTENTS

CHAPTER ONE

CHANGES AROUND THE GLOBE

Flooded cities. Deadly heat waves. Roaring forest fires. Polar bears stranded by melted ice. **Droughts**. Summer flowers blooming in winter. What on Earth is going on?

Earth is warming. A 2017 United States government report concluded that from 1901 to 2016, the average global temperature increased by about 1.8 degrees Fahrenheit (1 degree Celsius).

Polar bears hunt by waiting on floating sea ice for seals to surface. Melting ice means they have fewer opportunities to find seals. Many bears are going hungry.

Rescuers assisted residents after severe floods hit communities in England in December 2015.

Average Global Temperature

Temperatures aren't rising at the same rate everywhere on Earth. But scientists have tracked temperatures on land and sea to calculate the worldwide average temperature increase. The measurements show Earth is getting hotter overall.

Scientists warn that wildfires will become more severe as Earth warms.

This warming causes changes in the world's **climate**. For example, warmer air holds more water, allowing bigger storms to develop. Many areas are receiving more rain than normal. Floods have become more frequent and severe.

Köppen Climate Types of the World

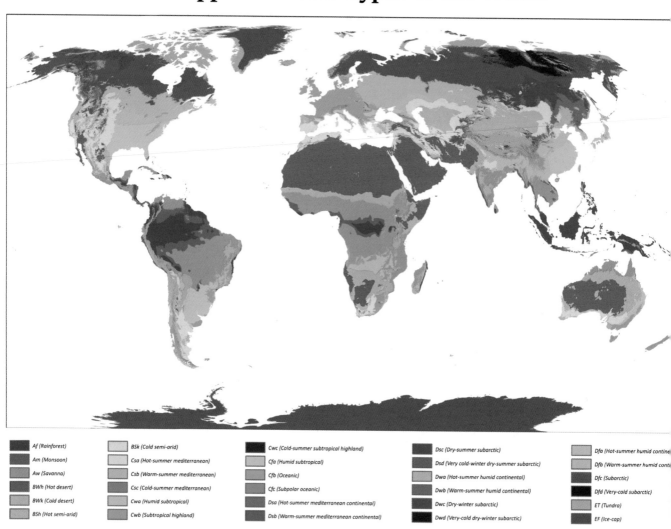

Af (Rainforest)	BSk (Cold semi-arid)	Cwc (Cold-summer subtropical highland)	Dsc (Dry-summer subarctic)	Dfa (Hot-summer humid contine
Am (Monsoon)	Csa (Hot-summer mediterranean)	Cfa (Humid subtropical)	Dsd (Very cold-winter dry-summer subarctic)	Dfb (Warm-summer humid conti
Aw (Savanna)	Csb (Warm-summer mediterranean)	Cfb (Oceanic)	Dwa (Hot-summer humid continental)	Dfc (Subarctic)
BWh (Hot desert)	Csc (Cold-summer mediterranean)	Cfc (Subpolar oceanic)	Dwb (Warm-summer humid continental)	Dfd (Very-cold subarctic)
BWk (Cold desert)	Cwa (Humid subtropical)	Dsa (Hot-summer mediterranean continental)	Dwc (Dry-winter subarctic)	ET (Tundra)
BSh (Hot semi-arid)	Cwb (Subtropical highland)	Dsb (Warm-summer mediterranean continental)	Dwd (Very-cold dry-winter subarctic)	EF (Ice-cap)

Temperature Change in the Last 50 Years

(2014-2018 Average vs. 1951-1980 Baseline)

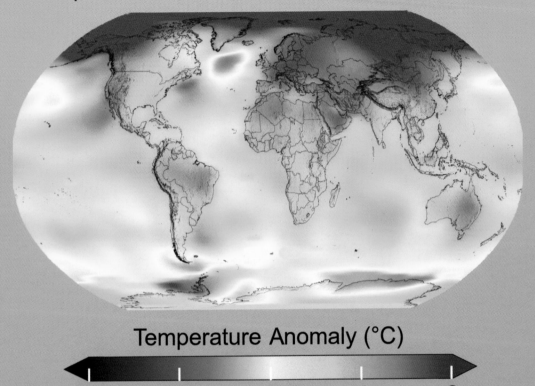

Temperature Anomaly (°C)

-2   -1   0   +1   +2

This NASA (National Aeronautics and Space Administration) map shows changes in average temperatures around the globe. Colors indicate degrees of difference (higher or lower) between the baseline average temperatures (1951 to 1980), and recent average temperatures from 2014 to 2018.

Global Warming or Climate Change?

Global warming is one aspect of the broader pattern of worldwide climate change. The concept of climate includes temperature, precipitation, wind, humidity, and storms. Scientists use both terms (global warming and climate change) to describe different aspects of Earth's changing conditions.

Some places are drier than usual. Hotter temperatures and longer summers dry soils and contribute to drier forests, which burn more easily. Since the 1980s, forest fires have grown larger and harder to control in the western United States and Canada. Shifting weather patterns have brought droughts to the Middle East, Asia, Africa, and elsewhere.

The oceans are warming too. Warmer water expands, so oceans are rising. In addition, **polar** ice sheets and mountain glaciers are melting, further raising sea levels. The world's oceans have risen four to eight inches (10 to 20 centimeters) in the past century.

In this NASA graphic, red indicates the greatest sea level rises over the past two decades. Orange and yellow show smaller rises. Blue means the water level is unchanged or lower.

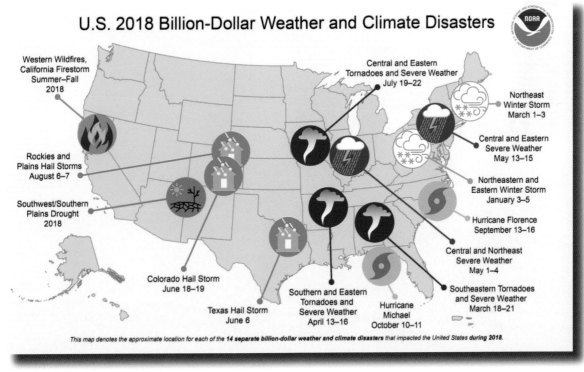

In recent years, weather disasters have been more frequent, more severe, and more costly. This is caused by a combination of circumstances. Many can be traced to the effects of climate change.

Many are alarmed by these changes. Biologists observe that plants, animals, and ecosystems are suffering. Farmers face rainfall and temperature changes that damage their crops. Coastal cities see higher floodwaters.

Climate skeptics, or climate change deniers, dispute such concerns. They argue that changes in climate are a normal part of Earth's history. Some point to freezing winter temperatures and big blizzards and conclude the climate can't be warming. This argument, however, ignores evidence of long-term temperature trends.

Tom Coburn, a Republican and former U.S. Senator from Oklahoma, said in 2013, "I am a global warming denier. I don't deny that."

Protesters in Santa Rosa, California, supported environmental awareness during Earth Day's March for Science.

Some skeptics, such as Scott Pruitt, former head of the U.S. Environmental Protection Agency (EPA), suggest warmer weather could be good for people. Yet the U.S. government's *Fourth National Climate Assessment*, released in November 2018, explains how global warming brings heat waves, air and water pollution, food shortages, increased disease, and other threats to human health.

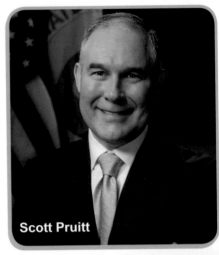

Scott Pruitt

Meanwhile, U.S. policies responding to climate change have been inconsistent, changing as leadership shifts between the Republican and Democratic parties.

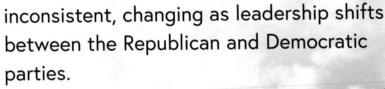

EPA headquarters are in Washington, D.C. According to the agency's website, "EPA research improves knowledge of the health and environment effects of climate change."

CHAPTER TWO

CARBON AND CLIMATE CHANGE

At least 97 percent of scientists studying climate agree that human actions have caused rapid global warming. Since the Industrial Revolution began in the late 1700s, humans have added billions of tons of **greenhouse gases** (GHGs) to the air. These gases—primarily carbon dioxide, methane, and nitrous oxide—hold heat in Earth's atmosphere, warming the planet like a greenhouse warms plants.

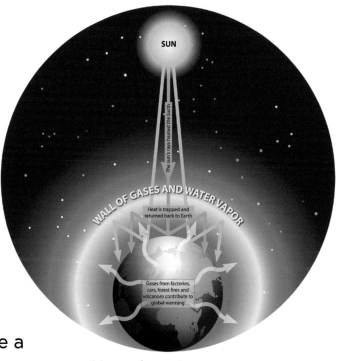

A layer of greenhouse gases around Earth acts like a blanket to hold the sun's heat in the atmosphere.

Most GHGs come from burning fossil fuels such as coal, oil, and natural gas to produce electricity and transport people and freight. Transportation and industry are major sources of carbon dioxide. Methane is generated by oil and gas production, by farm animals, and by trash rotting in landfills. Nitrous oxide comes mainly from agriculture and burning fossil fuels.

For 400,000 years before the Industrial Revolution, carbon dioxide levels in the atmosphere were stable, ranging between 200 and 280 parts per million (ppm). In 2013, the carbon dioxide level reached 400 ppm for the first time ever recorded. It continues to increase.

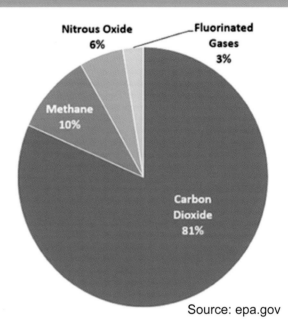

U.S. Greenhouse Gas Emissions in 2016

Nitrous Oxide
6%

Fluorinated Gases
3%

Methane
10%

Carbon Dioxide
81%

Source: epa.gov

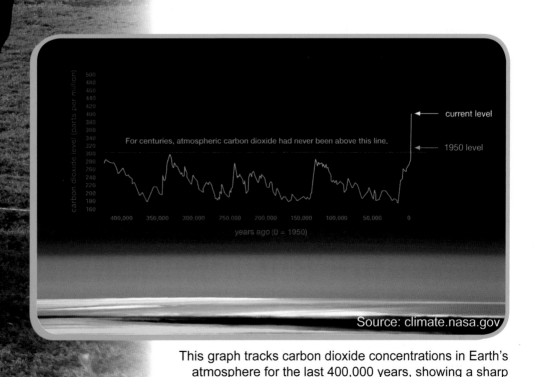

For centuries, atmospheric carbon dioxide had never been above this line.

current level

1950 level

carbon dioxide level (parts per million)

years ago (0 = 1950)

Source: climate.nasa.gov

This graph tracks carbon dioxide concentrations in Earth's atmosphere for the last 400,000 years, showing a sharp increase in the last century.

Ice Cores

Paleoclimatologists study polar ice to learn about the long-ago atmosphere. This ice formed from snow falling over thousands of years. Deeper ice is older. Scientists have drilled ice core samples more than 2.1 miles (3.4 kilometers) deep. Bubbles in the ice provide air samples, some hundreds of thousands of years old.

Scientists predict that as GHG concentrations rise, they will further disrupt the climate. Extreme weather events will continue. The oceans will become more **acidic**. Humans will face hunger and disease. Plants and animals will become extinct.

When ocean temperatures rise, corals expel algae living in their tissues, resulting in coral bleaching (shown above) and leaving reefs vulnerable to disease.

Ocean Acidification

Since the Industrial Revolution, the oceans have absorbed hundreds of billions of tons of carbon dioxide. The gas dissolves, forming carbonic acid. This makes the water more acidic. Ocean acidification makes it difficult for marine animals to grow shells, and it kills coral reefs.

Some dispute these predictions, arguing that changes in the climate are part of Earth's natural cycle of ice ages and warming. While it's true that natural events such as volcanic eruptions can affect climate, scientists have concluded that these don't explain this century's large changes. Other skeptics say human beings will adapt to new conditions. Scientists point out, however, that such adaptation takes many years, and that humans are well adapted to the more stable climate that existed for most of human development.

CHAPTER THREE

CAN CLIMATE CHANGE BE STOPPED?

Fighting climate change means slowing the increase of GHGs in the atmosphere by reducing new **emissions** and removing GHGs from the air. The most direct way to cut GHG emissions is to burn less fossil fuel. Renewable energy sources such as solar and wind power, which produce few or no GHGs, can replace fossil fuels. Electric cars create zero emissions (though producing the electricity they use may generate GHGs). Making homes, appliances, and factories more energy efficient also reduces emissions.

Wind turbines use the power of wind to generate electricity. "Wind power is an important part of America's energy strategy," said U.S. Energy Secretary Rick Perry in 2019.

The oil and gas industries oppose regulations aimed at cutting fossil fuel use. They say renewable energy sources are not enough. They're concerned that the proposed rules would reduce their profits. They also argue that cutting fossil fuel consumption puts workers—coal miners, oil rig operators, and others—out of jobs. But many point out that the renewable energy economy offers good jobs with a more sustainable future.

Photovoltaic solar panels convert energy from the sun into electricity. Sun power can also be used to dry clothes, heat water, or cook food.

Agriculture also produces GHGs. Commercial livestock operations that raise meat—especially beef—are major methane sources. Some people advocate eating less beef to combat climate change. Some farmers are exploring ways to reduce emissions by changing what they feed cattle and by limiting chemical fertilizers (which produce carbon dioxide and nitrous oxide). Cutting food waste—sending less to dumps—would save energy used in food production and also reduce methane emissions from decomposing trash.

Burp-Free Cows?

Farm animals produce about 14 percent of greenhouse gas emissions. Cattle pass gas in large amounts, and their flatulence and belches contain methane which has a stronger warming effect than carbon dioxide. Scientists are trying to breed cattle that burp—and fart!—less.

People are also working to remove carbon from the atmosphere. Plants do this naturally by absorbing carbon dioxide. So preserving forests and planting trees helps reduce carbon in the air. Further, new technology could separate out the carbon dioxide from factories or power plants and inject it into the ground.

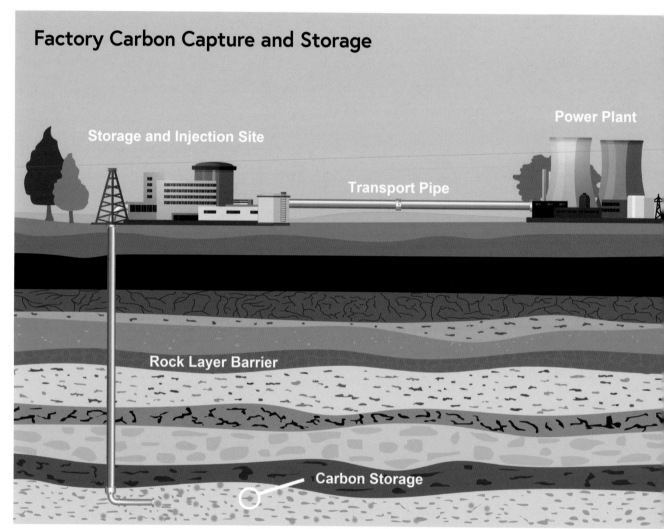

Factory Carbon Capture and Storage

Storage and Injection Site

Power Plant

Transport Pipe

Rock Layer Barrier

Carbon Storage

Carbon capture and storage (CCS) means transporting CO_2 in liquid form to natural chambers deep undergroun This technology has the potential to capture at least 90 percent of industrial CO_2 emissions.

Going Green

Know your footprint
A carbon footprint is the total amount of carbon emissions an entity is responsible for. Know your impact so you can reduce it.

Travel less
Traveling, especially flights, can be a big source of carbon emissions. Cut your traveling to reduce CO_2.

Save water
Water is the single most important substance we have on Earth. Look for ways to reduce water usage.

Save energy
Electricity is by far the biggest single source of carbon emissions. Reducing your energy usage will also save you money.

Plant trees
Trees are a quick solution because they directly absorb carbon dioxide. Plant one today.

Choose organic
Organic products are not only better for our health but also better for our environment. Switch over today.

Recycle more
Recycle waste to keep it out of landfills and so reduce carbon emissions. Choose bio-degradable products.

Create awareness
People don't act because they don't know. Be informed and create awareness. We need everyone's help.

What's Your Carbon Footprint?

A person's carbon footprint measures their contribution to climate change—the GHGs their activities generate. Burning one gallon (3.8 liters) of gasoline, for example, produces about 19 pounds (8.6 kilograms) of carbon dioxide. Individuals and businesses can use carbon footprint calculators to understand and reduce their impacts.

CHAPTER FOUR

THE GLOBAL RESPONSE

In 1988, the Intergovernmental Panel on Climate Change (IPCC) of the United Nations (UN) was created to **assess** and report on global climate science. In 1992, the UN Framework Convention on Climate Change (UNFCCC), an agreement to cooperate in controlling GHGs, was finalized. Virtually all nations on Earth approved this agreement.

Earth Summit

The 1992 UNFCCC agreement was reached in Rio de Janeiro, Brazil, at a UN conference that many called the Earth Summit. In addition to the climate change agreement, nations in attendance also pledged to:

- *Take inventories of their plants and wild animals and protect endangered species*

- *Clean up the environment and encourage environmentally sound development*

- *Preserve the world's rapidly vanishing tropical rainforests*

Hurricane Harvey hit the greater Houston, Texas, area in 2017. It resulted in about 125 billion dollars in damage, caused more than 80 deaths, and made thousands of people homeless.

Climate Refugees

Each year from 2008 to 2018, an average of 24 million people were displaced from their homes by floods, droughts, and other environmental and weather disasters. Communities from Louisiana to the Pacific island nation of Kiribati are sinking beneath rising waters, and drought-related food shortages threaten millions more.

A massive tsunami triggered by a huge earthquake left much of northeastern Japan destroyed in 2011. Scientists are studying the relationship between climate disruption and increased earthquakes and tsunamis.

Under President Bill Clinton, the United States signed the Kyoto Protocol in 1998. In 2006, former president Clinton made a speech stating that climate change is the greatest threat facing the world's security.

Under President George W. Bush, the U.S. abandoned the Kyoto Protocol. Bush acknowledged that something should be done about climate change, but pointed out that there were uncertainties about how fast the climate was changing and what effects new policies might have.

The countries signing the UNFCCC meet annually to discuss their progress. At the 1997 meeting in Kyoto, Japan, they created the Kyoto Protocol. This agreement required **developed** countries to make specified cuts in GHG emissions. U.S. President Bill Clinton signed the Kyoto agreement, but Congress didn't approve it. In 2001, under President George W. Bush, the U.S. dropped out of the agreement.

Pictured here are delegates at the 2015 Paris, France,
meeting of the United Nations Climate Change Conference.

The 2015 UNFCCC climate conference was held in Paris, France. In the resulting Paris Agreement, the United States and more than 190 other countries agreed to reduce emissions to hold the overall average global temperature increase to below 3.6 degrees Fahrenheit (2 degrees Celsius). They also agreed to try to limit the increase to 2.7 degrees Fahrenheit (1.5 degrees Celsius) to avoid more severe effects.

In 2012, Donald Trump tweeted that climate change was a hoax. In 2018, he said he did not believe it was a hoax, but that he would not take actions that would harm American economic interests.

In 2017, President Donald Trump announced the United States would withdraw from the Paris Agreement because he wanted to put America's interests first. He said the agreement was bad for the U.S. economy, in particular the fossil fuel industry. He complained the agreement was unfair because it required developed nations to assist developing nations such as India in reducing emissions.

World leaders criticized the U.S. action and vowed to continue cutting GHGs. U.S. economists warned that failing to control climate change could cost the U.S. trillions of dollars in increased health care and costs related to flooding, fires, and other disasters.

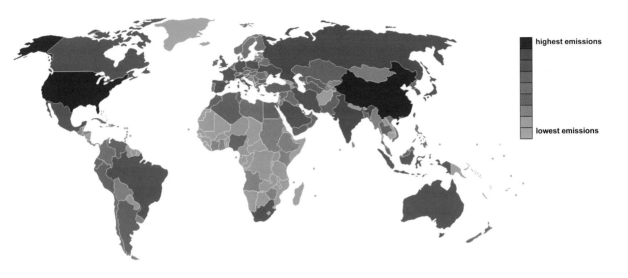

highest emissions

lowest emissions

This map shows the world's carbon dioxide emissions by country. Data in recent years has shown the U.S. and China to be the two highest emitters.

IPCC Warning

In October 2018, the IPCC issued a special report about the effects of global warming. It concluded that major, immediate GHG cuts are needed to avoid severe environmental damage. Despite its announced withdrawal from the Paris Agreement, the United States approved the IPCC report.

China has increased its production of electric cars and has installed many electric charging stations.

China uses large numbers of coal-fired power plants and is the world's largest emitter of GHGs. But China, too, has taken steps to reduce emissions. It leads the world in sales of electric cars, is a major developer of solar energy, and is planting trees.

Rapid industrialization in China led to serious air pollution in cities such as Beijing, pictured here.

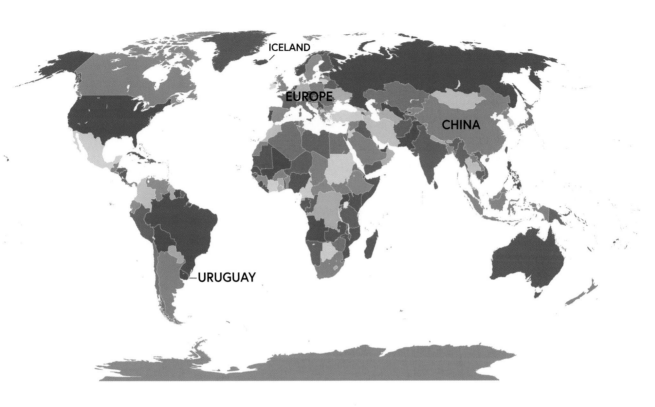

The European Union has adopted **regional** standards restricting GHG emissions and supporting renewable energy. Many other countries are also taking important steps. For example, almost all of Iceland's energy is renewable. Uruguay generates 97 to 100 percent of its electricity from renewable sources. Global leaders are not giving up.

CHAPTER FIVE

U.S. CLIMATE POLICIES

RENEWABLE

U.S. **federal** climate policies have varied. President Barack Obama's administration (2009–2017) worked to reduce GHG emissions. It required emissions reductions from power plants and cars, halted new coal mining leases on federal lands, protected forests, and invested in renewable energy.

In 2015, Obama pledged to "make sure American leadership drives international action" to address the climate change crisis.

In 2017, President Donald Trump started reversing these policies. When oil and gas companies asked for expanded drilling on federal lands, his administration agreed. Trump said he wanted to save jobs in the fossil fuel industry. The Trump White House revoked rules that protected wildlife, allowing more oil and gas drilling.

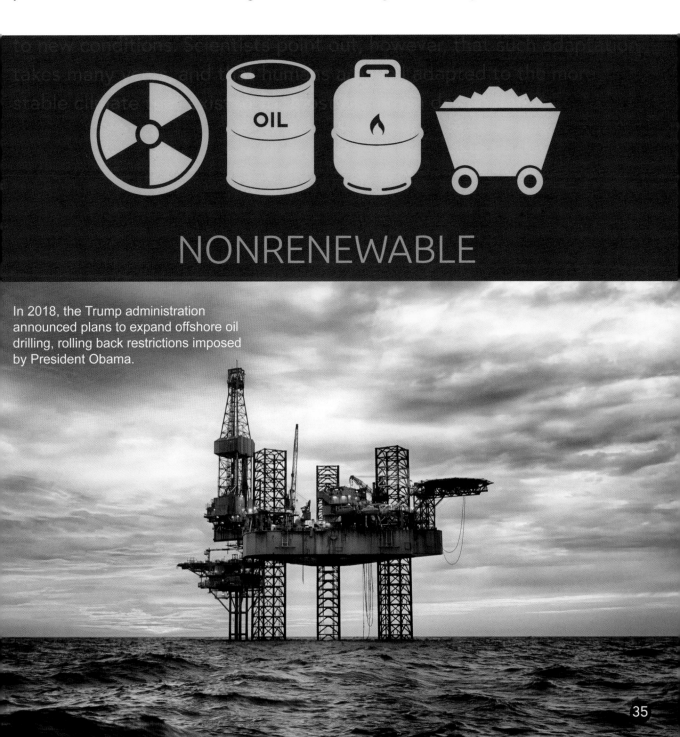

NONRENEWABLE

In 2018, the Trump administration announced plans to expand offshore oil drilling, rolling back restrictions imposed by President Obama.

Taking It to the Courts

In 2015, 21 young people sued the U.S. government, arguing that the failure to fight climate change **violates** their rights. In *Juliana v. United States,* they sought a court order telling the government to act. In 2018, the Supreme Court allowed their case to go to trial.

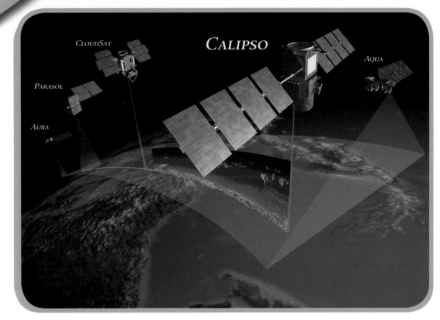

NASA and its international partners operate an array of satellites that record measurements of Earth and its changing climate.

Federal agencies including NASA continue to conduct and publish important climate research. Congress has required the government to study and report on climate change and its impacts. Although the Trump administration wanted to cut climate research, Congress continued to fund it.

In addition, the governors of more than 20 U.S. states joined together as the United States Climate Alliance. They committed to reduce GHG emissions consistent with the Paris Agreement goals. These states believe controlling climate change is good for the planet and for their economies.

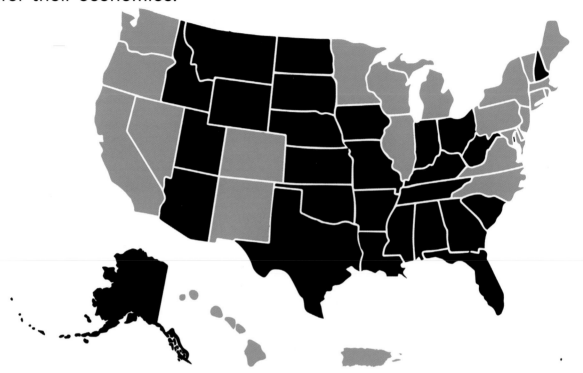

As of April 2019, the 24 members of the U.S. Climate Alliance were: California, Colorado, Connecticut, Delaware, Hawaii, Illinois, Maine, Maryland, Massachusetts, Michigan, Minnesota, Nevada, New Jersey, New Mexico, New Y North Carolina, Oregon, Pennsylvania, Puerto Rico, Rhode Island, Vermont, Virginia, Washington, and Wisconsin

Jim Bridenstine became

Listening to the Science

In 2013, Republican Congressman Jim Bridenstine denied that humans caused climate change. In 2018, after being appointed NASA's administrator, Bridenstine acknowledged: "The climate is changing. I also know that we human beings are contributing to it in a major way." His views evolved after he studied

CHAPTER SIX

CLIMATE ADAPTATION

Climate change is creating a "new normal." Whether national leaders deny that climate change exists or fight to control it, local communities must deal with its effects. They're initiating climate adaptation measures.

Worsening floods have overcome seawalls and levees, and communities are seeking more effective flood control measures. Building new homes and businesses farther from shorelines, or moving existing structures away from flood-prone areas, can protect them from flooding. Creating new **wetlands** and open spaces is a good way to prevent flooding because these areas absorb excess water.

Climate changes have also made wildfires more severe. Firefighting experts recommend creating healthier forests that can resist fires. They suggest planting trees that are suited to survive new climate conditions and controlling insects that weaken trees.

Wetlands filter contamination out of water, provide wildlife habitat, and absorb rainfall to prevent flooding. New wetlands can be created by planting water-loving plants and building berms to hold water.

Villagers created these tall, cone-shaped ice stupas, or artificial glaciers, to store water in the high desert of Ladakh, India.

Rural Innovation

In India's high mountains, rural communities traditionally rely on mountain glaciers for drinking water. With those glaciers disappearing, some have created

Adding nets and thorn-covered branches to artificial glaciers allows ice to form more quickly.

artificial glaciers. In winter, people pipe water from streams to create tall mounds of ice. In springtime, the ice melts, freeing the stored water for drinking and watering crops.

Farmers facing crop failures are switching to new crops better suited to new conditions. Some are installing expensive irrigation systems or looking for new water sources. Some are even using seawater after removing salt from the water through evaporation.

How To Desalt Saline Water

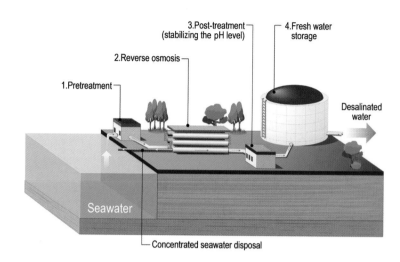

As people confront increasing evidence of the dangers posed by climate change, the calls for action have also increased. Although the debate in the United States continues, nations around the globe have committed to reducing GHGs. Many continue to hope that people can control climate change by working together. As former UN climate chief Christiana Figueres has said, "When we decide on a task to be done, no matter how daunting it may seem at the beginning, we are able to unleash human ingenuity and human innovative capacity."

People (including you!) can address climate change by many means, including by reducing energy use and cutting GHG emissions.

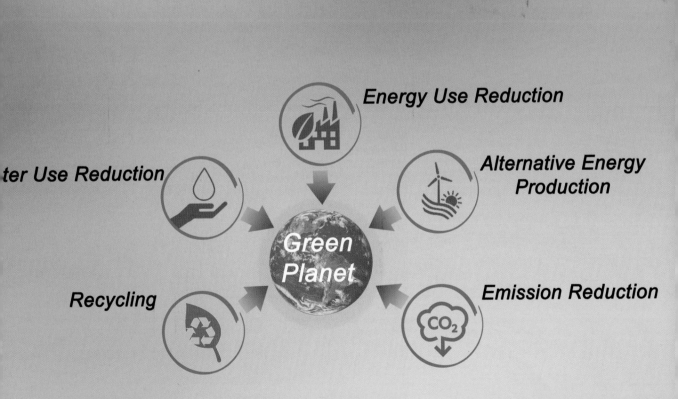

PRACTICE PREPARING FOR A DEBATE

People explain issues and solve problems through discussion. Debates are formal discussions about an issue. Debate participants present facts they have gathered from reliable sources. They present this information as they try to convince listeners that their opinions about an issue are correct.

Supplies

- paper
- pencil
- books on your topic and/or internet access

Directions:

1. Decide the topic you will research.

2. Write a question that will shape your debate. Example: Should religion be taught in public schools?

3. Write your proposition or opposition statement. Proposition example: Religion should be taught in public schools. Opposition example: Religion should not be taught in public schools.

4. Research your topic using a variety of sources. Make a list of the facts you find and note the source of each fact next to it.

5. Practice presenting your argument.

6. Flip the script! Follow steps 1–5 again, this time preparing with facts that support the other side.

Bonus: Form a debate club with your friends. Assign a new topic regularly. Give each person equal time to present their arguments.

Glossary

acidic (uh-SID-ik): containing acid, a type of chemical that is able to dissolve metals; the opposite of basic or alkaline

assess (uh-SES): to evaluate or judge the condition of something

climate (KLYE-mit): typical weather conditions over a long period of time

developed (di-VEL-uhpd): having high levels of wealth, technology, and industry, as in developed countries, also called industrialized countries

droughts (droutz): long periods without normal rainfall, often leading to water shortages

emissions (i-MISH-uhnz): releases, especially of harmful gases, into the atmosphere

federal (FED-ur-uhl): relating to the central or national government in a system in which individual states also have their own laws and governments, as in the U.S. federal government

greenhouse gases (GHGs) (GREEN-hous GAS-iz): substances in the atmosphere such as carbon dioxide and methane that contribute to the warming of Earth through the greenhouse effect

polar (POH-lur): related to the icy regions at Earth's North Pole and South Pole

regional (REE-juhn-uhl): relating to a specific district or territory of a city, country, or continent

violates (VYE-uh-layts): fails to respect

wetlands (WET-landz): natural areas with a great deal of moisture in the soil, such as marshes, swamps, and bayous

Index

Text-Dependent Questions

1. What are some changes caused by higher average temperatures on Earth?

2. Why did scientists conclude that GHGs caused climate change?

3. How does agriculture contribute to GHG emissions?

4. What is the purpose of the Paris Agreement?

5. What are some examples of climate adaptation?

Extension Activity

What is your carbon footprint? That's the amount of carbon dioxide your activities contribute to the atmosphere. Use an online calculator to estimate yours. Then identify some ways you could reduce your footprint. Can you develop an action plan to reduce your family's carbon footprint?

Carbon footprint calculators vary. Here are three online options that can help you estimate your impact.

U.S. EPA:
https://www.epa.gov/ghgemissions/household-carbon-footprint-calculator

The Greens (Zero Footprint Youth Calculator):
http://www.meetthegreens.org/features/carbon-calculator.html

Conservation International:
https://www.conservation.org/act/carboncalculator/calculate-your-carbon-footprint.aspx#/.

Bibliography

Bloomberg, Michael, and Carl Pope, *Climate of Hope: How Cities, Businesses, and Citizens Can Save the Planet*, New York: St. Martin's Press, 2017.

Burke, Marshall, W. Matthew Davis, and Noah Diffenbaugh, "Large Potential Reduction in Economic Damages under UN Mitigation Targets," *Nature* 557 (May 23, 2018): 549-553.

Halper, Evan, "Trump Administration's Rewrite of Clean Power Plan Will Be a Boon to the Coal Industry," *Los Angeles Times*, Aug. 20, 2018.

Intergovernmental Panel on Climate Change, https://www.ipcc.ch, (accessed January 5, 2019).

Koren, Marina, "Trump's NASA Chief: 'I Fully Believe and Know the Climate is Changing,'" *The Atlantic*, May 17, 2018.

McCarthy, Shawn, "Christiana Figueres: Passionate—and Impatient—about Climate," *The Globe and Mail*, Oct. 10, 2014.

Mooney, Chris, Juliet Eilperin, and Brady Dennis, "Trump Administration Releases Report Finding 'No Convincing Alternative Explanation' for Climate Change." *Washington Post*, Nov. 3, 2017.

National Aeronautics and Space Administration (NASA) Global Climate Change: Vital Signs of the Planet, "Climate Change: How Do We Know?" https://climate.nasa.gov/evidence/. (last updated April 29, 2019).

Shaftel, Holly, "The Scientific Method and Climate Change: How Scientists Know," NASA Global Climate Change, Vital Signs of the Planet, June 6, 2018, https://climate.nasa.gov/news/2743/the-scientific-method-and-climate-change-how-scientists-know/

United States Climate Alliance, https://www.usclimatealliance.org/, (accessed January 3, 2019).

United States Environmental Protection Agency, "Climate Change Indicators in the United States," https://www.epa.gov/climate-indicators, (last updated June 22, 2017).

United States Global Change Research Program, *Fourth National Climate Assesssment Vol. II: Impacts, Risks, and Adaptation in the United States*, https://nca2018.globalchange.gov/, (accessed Jan. 3, 2019).

About the Author

Christy Mihaly writes books and articles for young people, including titles about science, nature, technology, and math. She studied environmental policy at Dartmouth College and law at the University of California, Berkeley. She spent more than two decades working as an environmental lawyer in California before moving with her family to rural Vermont, where she currently enjoys writing under the supervision of her dog and cat. You can visit her website at www.christymihaly.com.

www.rourkeeducationalmedia.com

PHOTO CREDITS: Cover: drawings of faces © topform | Shutterstock.com, photo © kpboonjit; Pages 4-5 flooded city Editorial credit: PhilMacDPhoto / Shutterstock.com, forest fire © Christian Roberts-Olsen, polar bear © Chase Dekker, illustration © Jurik Peter; Pages 8-9 cracked earth © Sunny Forest; Page 10 © Edgar G Biehle, page 11 Tom Coburn Editorial credit: Christopher Halloran / Shutterstock.com, protesters Editorial credit: Kim Wilson / Shutterstock.com; Page 13 © asadykov; Pages 14-15 cows © Rudmer Zwerver; Pages 16-17 © RavenEyePhoto; Page 18 coral © MYP Studio, volcano © solarseven; Pages 20-21 wind turbines © Volodymyr Burdiak, solar panels © Diyana Dimitrova, electric cars © sungsu han; Pages 22-23 cows © Budimir Jevtic, hands with animal feed © Dewald Kirsten, food waste © nito, cow illustration © M-SUR; page 25 carbon footprint sidebar © Leon Skinner; Pages 26-27 earthquake damage © Smallcreative, flood © Trong Nguyen; Page 31 cityscape © alphaspirit; Pages 32-33 boy © Hung Chung Chih, electric car Editorial credit: EQRoy / Shutterstock.com, world map © ekler; Pages 34-35 illustrations © mjaud, oil rig © Lukasz Z; Pages 36 -37 protesters © DisobeyArt, girl with signEditorial credit: Luoxi / Shutterstock.com; Page 38 map of United States © iiierlok_xolms, Page 39 © ParabolStudio; Page 41 artificial glacier photos Editorial credit: Naveen Macro / Shutterstock.com; Page 42 diagram © Designua, photo © Satyrenko; Page 43 © arka38. All images from Shutterstock.com except: Pages 6-7 climate map © Adam Peterson https://creativecommons.org/licenses/©-sa/4.0/deed.en, temperature change diagram page 7, map of Earth page 9 courtesy of NASA, bottom grpahic courtesy of NASA; Pages 12 EPA building Public Domain image © Moreau1, Scott Pruitt and EPA logo courtesy of U.S. Government, Page 13 Greenhouse Effect ID 23247424 © Lukaves | Dreamstime.com; Page 15 Pie Chart courtesy of EPA, graph from Data: National Oceanic and Atmospheric Administration with some description adapted from the Scripps CO2 Program Page 16 National Ice Core Laboratory Public Domain image Made available © Eric Cravens, Assistant Curator, National Ice Core Lab.; Page 24 © BD Pub; Page 26 Map Public Domain image; Page 28 Bill Clinton and George Bush and page 30 Donald Trump courtesy of U.S. federal government, Page 29 © Presidencia de la República Mexicana https://creativecommons.org/licenses/©/2.0/, Page 31 © Distantbody / Jrockley https://creativecommons.org/licenses/©-sa/3.0/deed.en; Page 38 Jim Bridenstine courtesy of NASA; Page 40 courtesy of Erika Sanchez-Chopitea, USGS Western Ecological Research Center.

Edited by: Kim Thompson
Produced by Blue Door Education for Rourke Educational Media. Cover and interior design by: Jennifer Dydyk

Library of Congress PCN Data

Defining and Discussing Climate Change / Christy Mihaly
(Shaping the Debate)
ISBN 978-1-73161-475-9 (hard cover)
ISBN 978-1-73161-282-3 (soft cover)
ISBN 978-1-73161-580-0 (e-Book)
ISBN 978-1-73161-685-2 (e-Pub)
Library of Congress Control Number: 2019932394

Rourke Educational Media
Printed in the United States of America,
North Mankato, Minnesota